Climbing Glass

Lyle Closs

Second edition, November 2020

First edition published by Blurb, April 2009

This book is dedicated to the friends who have corresponded with me over the years and helped keep me thrashing a keyboard, especially Dick Hain, Christopher Race and Peter Jackson; and to my Australian climbing partners and great friends Ian Lewis, Bryan Kennedy (RIP), Ben Maddison, Bob McMahon (RIP), Peter Jackson, Bob Bull, Mikl Law, Tom Williams and Greg Mortimer. If only we could have climbed together more often.

My sincere thanks to the legend Chris Baxter for considerate and sensible editing of the first edition. R.I.P.

Bob Bull, Mendelt Tillema, Lyle Closs, Don Holmes after a day
at Sunshine Possibilities, Tasmania, 1972

Contents

Bob McMahon, Peter Jackson, Reg Williams.
Below Stacks Bluff, Tasmania, 1971

Appeal for the unknown first climber

There are just a few people who are important to me. Bob Bull, who led the first ascent of Eurydice at Mt Arapiles. A sound record of misbehaviour in his youth. Lovely family now. Farm in the mountains behind Hobart. Excellent record collection. Great bloke by the fire when the rain's pissing down on the cold Tassie hills, a glass of Guinness warming in your fist.

Don Holmes for example. Died of a cancer a few years back. Fought it monumentally for many years. Drank a lot with me and the lads a long time ago. His name is on a few routes, but you don't know him. And that's frustrating.

Reg Williams. A great climber and bushman. Stutters. A very important person in the lives of many. On the first ascent of Emperor at Mt Buffalo. Led the first ascent of Missing Link at Arapiles. Not just initials in a book. Raising his kids. Making perfect replica steam trains for Christ's sake. But this story annoys you.

Peter Jackson, teacher, powerhouse of suburban Hobart, man of many visions, early pioneer of Arapiles, searcher ever since. Lots of climbs with his name on, and many line drawings without peer, but do you sense how I feel here?

Have I lost you?

Me? I did a few new routes, knew a few people, made a certain short term impression.

But what does 'First climbed: L. Closs' mean to anyone? Nothing, I suspect.

So what the hell use is this strange appendage at the bottom of each route description? Why bother recording the first climbers if no-one knows who those people are, and no-one cares?

If it says 'First climbed: D. Whillans, J. Brown' now that means something because you've read the biographies, seen the movie, analysed the photographs. There's some response drilled up from the core of the mind. There's some encouragement there to resurrect the mythology...

My mythology, now. What do you know of that if you haven't read the Climbers Club of Tasmania newsletters and copies of *Thrutch,* the Australian climbing magazine from the late 60s, early 70s? You probably never knew they existed.

My mythology involves the people above among many others and is wreathed in past mists, lit bright with the sharp rays of younger perception - all that crap.

And all of these important climbers I have mentioned – each has or had his own mythology in which I am but a passing shade drifting through and past. To themselves they are mythologically central.

Mythology is just distorted memory of course. It is not real and deserves less credence than it is allowed. Pathos, also, insists on playing a part.

And it does seem a little pathetic that we must force our meagre mythologies on to the small guidebook page. Other climbers thumb them to find the way to a present, a future climbing enjoyment. Not to create a wistful remembrance of days long past. Not to re-create that day when fingers first caressed this rock.

Other climbers only care for the great climbers, the greater myths. They don't care for me or my aging or gone friends.

They certainly don't have, nor do they want, the capacity to know of our feelings at the time we scaled those heights.

Dammit, there is no art in any of it. The climb descriptions are as much descriptive of human emotion as the remembrance columns in the Sunday papers.

And when they climb our climbs, well, the physical surroundings are roughly the same, but the actions are different, and of course their feelings as they climb are new, personally exclusive.

But our feelings, my feelings, on those first ascents on what were then rarely visited cliffs! Now there is something like art, something like real dreams in flood.

To soar where none had been before! Those dreams are now gone though, reliant on the pathos of passed time for their imperfect resurrection.

Those little words 'First climbed...' at the bottom of the route description are memorials to other men's dreams.

And perhaps your dreams are every bit as powerful or languorous as were those of the first to climb this climb.

But stop the mental static a moment before you approach the eternally patient stone and think of those who first dreamed the dream.

Even if they no longer breathe, at least, that day, they dreamed where no man had dreamed before. It's a thing worthy of the gods. A breath upon the window of eternity.

And as the printing of the names of the first to climb the route is a memorial to other men's dreams, to climb that climb is to lie in another man's grave.

The grave may be the same. But it was not dug for you.

...

Lyle Closs, Karl Prinz after the first ascent of Carlyle -
Federation Peak, Tasmania, 1972

Time—a reappraisal

Dear Mother

The twitch of a fibrositised muscle in my shoulder annoys me intensely. I am reading history books and wishing there was something else. I have finally finished reading the world's array of literature and am naturally a little depressed.

Where does one turn having achieved such a goal?

History is a drab and annoying subject. At least in literature there are endings. There is only one course taken and only one set of options expressed. I take some pleasure from the finality of it. At the last page, though the novel might have been dull, one has seen a creation pass definitely, or more importantly, finitely, before one's eyes. History is so open to drab interpretation.

In the excitement of approaching the end of my monstrous task I gave up climbing completely and so my muscle tone has withered slightly. I am back into training now. To miss out on the great journey would be unfortunate after so painful a lead-up.

I am climbing regularly now…but…but I feel affected. And I know that it is all to do with the completion of my awesome task of reading. How shall I relate this to you?

There are now no more books to read. Those that will come out in the future I can keep up with easily. And so I look about me and see…nothing.

I question the value of the exercise. Something has been achieved. But what? It seems too ephemeral. Gods created the world from the void. I see all new achievements as such. Placing abstracts into a vacuum.

As you know, every possible climb in the world has been done. Every crack and wall and spare meaningless little echo of space has been climbed, conquered by someone years ago in frenzies of exploration, expressing the need to be original, to feel a sense of freedom by taking it away from some piece of untouched cliff. Taking abstract emotions from concrete virginity. Passing on concrete desecration. Dying with the emotion forgotten but the desecration complete. As our climbing poet wrote:

"Now there is no virgin country,
Now there is no virgin rock,
Now there is no wild and heathen,
Now there are no chips off the old block.

We know all the holds."

If I were allowed a violence of reaction I would call out something like: 'ONCE THERE WERE OPEN SPACES UNTOUCHED BY CIVILISATION WHERE MEN COULD PROVE THEMSELVES. MOUNTAINS. RIVERS.'

You know.

Unfortunately, of course, we can't begrudge our ancestors their new routes. That would be absurd. But I feel I must pose the problem.

Total annihilation of the race may be the only answer. Then all this conquering will have been forgotten by the time another civilisation rises. People could do it all again. But the sacrifice is hardly worth the principle.

However. We have become a spiritless people. No new climbs to do. I am sick of speed climbing and other people's victories.

I look forward with wild anticipation to what may be found when our first exploration reaches the third planet. Titan has no joy for me anymore.

Your loving son.

...

Lyle Closs, Bob McMahon - Big Gun Pass, Tasmania, 1975

Chalk—a reappraisal

It's a typical Lindfield morning, on a typical Lindfield day in 1978. Giggling schoolgirls easily impressed by tight T-shirted sports-masters showing them the ropes. Young schoolboys imagining they are making an impression by swearing while standing at the very edge of the seven-metre drop.

The hermit in the cave down the hill lights a fire. Some guys are falling off the juggy overhang onto a brand new 11mm kernmantel rope, their shiny new boots uselessly scrabbling to shreds on the rock. An old guy at the bottom of Abseil Wall is directing someone move by move up the Turkey Route. A girl reads by the separate slab, oblivious to the carry-on. A 15-year-old, over and over again, attempts a climb on the slab.

I stumble down the steps with my pack and a wooden box with food, booze, book, sun cream, billy, jaffle iron, tape recorder, and a selection of tapes. I settle in near the base of Abseil Wall and from then on am continually asked if I am staying for the weekend. 'Yes I am. I will, in exactly ten minutes, erect my portable car tent with built-in sleeping-bag and plastic dunny for your elucidation and our mutual entertainment.' They blink and walk away.

I settle into a calm regime of red wine, Mauriac, camembert and Jatz. The sun beats peacefully on the hat I re-created from a pair of boots.

'One end is as good as the other where you're concerned.' (Anon, 1979.)

I cross my legs deliciously. A trite murmur ripples along the cliff-top. Aware but unperturbed I prepare myself, in my own way, for a personal assault on the best little practice cliff in Sydney.

After some 15 minutes of this relaxing of the social muscles, I rise and retire to the bush to relax the physical muscles with a little breathing. Necks crack audibly as they turn to watch my retiring, and the vapidity of their whispered comments follows me into the accepting trees. Oh, this world!

Eased from palm to arch after my yogic exercises, I breathe deeply and concentrate on the One Force. I have loosened the world-weary tendons that might otherwise have snapped with the tension of a thousand expectant eyes watching my every move, those fluid messages spelling out, hold by witless hold, the way to get up the climb, any climb.

'You couldn't climb a pygmy's shithouse.' (Boris Ellis, Frenchman's Cap, Feb '71.)

I approach the unsuspecting mob. I turn on George Thorogood and the Destroyers, very loud. Disappointed clucks can be just heard through the ripping slide guitar. Some people have no sensitivity, I think to myself, and ah, at last, I find the psychological muscles relaxed. I just need to feel rejected.

'I don't really feel like that. I just think people should have strong feelings about things.' (Mikl Law, May '79.)

So I swagger, with some exaggerated abandon, to the rock and impact up a few hopeless routes. Hopeless, because most of the awe-struck simpletons don't have a hope of getting up them. Most of the braying herd are then satisfied and drift away to their mindless pursuits.

'The world is full of mindless climbers.' (Ian Lewis, 1972.)

But pride comes before a retreat. Climb number XJ765 - variant c4 minus the finger-lock evades my rugged independent persistence. I have the right toe-tip, the left

Peter Borrer Closs - Lindfield, Sydney, 1987

heel hook, the right fingertip Lady Jane hold, but my left fingers don't seem to desire even a momentary affiliation with the sweat-crazed surface of the minuscule nodule necessary for the power assisted dyno with the right to the nail-cutter finger jug further out. To be embarrassingly succinct—I can't get up it. Caught between appearing not to be in control and the possibility of falling, I retreat with glum precision.

It's hard to be cool under such conditions. I can't stop myself from kicking the tape recorder, causing George to miss a chord. But I calm myself, and a sip of red eases the ache.

Unfortunately, the 15-year-old comes over from the slab and eases his pubescent simpering non-entiticular torso up the climb to the same position before also climbing back down to consider the move. But...he used chalk!

No-one with an ounce of pride uses chalk. It's an admission that you can't do the climb. You might as well bang in pitons.

'Chalk is just a state of mind.' (Myself, once.)

I head over to punch the drivelling little twerp in the face with the aim of asserting my threatened masculinity but, having escaped my zone of calm, I trip on my food box. Thrusting my hands before me I fall onto the juvenile, and my hands land in the offending bag of crushed white crutch. I revert to the vertical with abnormal haste. I cannot wipe the cruel clay from my previously unsullied fingers. I decide, dastardly fate, to try the climb again to clear the air of the critical thoughts seeping awkwardly from my fast dwindling public, and to cleanse my sullied skin.

I make the final move with ease! Curse my fatal far-reaching abilities.

Audience re-assured, 15-year-old in his necessarily diminutive place, I toss off the last of the reasonable but over-fruity 1974 Cabernet Shiraz.

'There's nothing like drinking so pleasant this side of the grave." (Charles Dibdin, 1745-1814.)

Ah, but the world has changed. A fearsome admittance sweeps me and shames me. It must be penned. Chalk makes a difference! I can no longer tread the screes of this forsaken continent without embarrassing white stains ruffling the rigid creases of my Mr John climbing trousers. I use the god-damned ethereal ointment, and I have come to care nothing of it. Why? Because my shameful and glorious ego over-rules my world-nurturing tendencies every time.

The cliffs are stained white. Curse the future and blame the present. Blame me if you care!

I snigger behind your backs. I posture before your very eyes. I can achieve more with chalk. Without it, you can not. Whose ego is in the best shape?

...

The use of chalk was unknown in Australian climbing before the mid-70s.

The great central line of The Wick, The Candlestick, Tasman Peninsula, Tasmania

10 years

Having spent my teens wildly fantasising of the climbing deeds I would perpetrate, I lost my early twenties in insecurity, looking for other, easier deeds on which to ride to glory. I am now carefully attempting to be rational with the remainder of my trembling, annoying years.

In 1971 though, I was very young - 17, working in a bank, living at home, climbing every weekend, virginally sincere and enthusiastic.

On a scheduled Climbers Club of Tasmania trip, Reg Williams, Mendelt Tillema, Col Hocking and I set out to climb the Candlestick from sea level for the first time. It had been reached just once previously by a monster Tyrolean traverse to a big ledge at two-thirds height.

With a large number of CCT viewers on the mainland, we swam across, set up gear, slowly climbed a long diagonal chimney to the big ledge, then stepped round the corner to follow the original line to the top.

We slept the night on the big ledge after warming ourselves with a fire, then in the morning we abseiled down and, by a strenuous diagonal prussik, got back to the mainland over boiling seas. Very tired, I spilt my only food on the dirt. Everyone laughed. I played it up a little.

It was a pleasant time, as were all those early days in the CCT—camaraderie prevailed, no egos, easy days.

In his write-up of the climb, Mendelt Tillema mentioned a line straight up the middle of the Candlestick. 'Maybe next year,' he wrote.

Ten years on it was still unclimbed. I was married and living in Sydney. During a visit to my family in Tasmania I persuaded Sydney lads Tom Williams and Steve McDowell to try the line with me.

...

The earth was damp from recent rains. The twisted eucalypts of the sea-sprayed peninsula dripped their saps to the charred earth. We headed down the hill, through the low scrub which tugs at loose clothes. Light winds pushed around the banksia.

We burst through the last stunted trees, stepped down the rocks and there was the Candlestick, the seas thankfully gentle in the avenue between it and the mainland.

The absurd Totem Pole poked in between them, a column of dolerite 70 metres high. I tried to remember my thoughts on first seeing the scene ten years earlier, but I couldn't. The swell seemed the same, the sky as blue, the bush no taller.

...

I remembered another visit though, five years before, in the swell of my bad years. I was unable to try hard at anything except retreat. Achieving an early, localised notoriety,

Ian Lewis and Kim Carrigan, 2nd ascent of the Totem Pole,
Tasman Peninsula, Tasmania, 1976

I had encouraged expectations that I would drink a lot, climb well, and behave like an animal. This fed my ego, and like a drug it turned against me, and I became unable to fulfil the expectations, except in drunken excess. I cowered emotionally when in front of the public I perceived, whether they were there or not.

For too long I led that unsatisfactory dance. I did no worthwhile climbing, nor anything else.

That time I had gone with many to climb, and to watch Kim Carrigan and Ian Lewis do the second ascent of the Totem Pole.

I watched. I attempted to climb the Candlestick's central line with Peter Treby. I followed the first pitch, the hardest as it turned out, then talked him into retreat in fear of the overhangs above. Sickening in the beautiful sun, I drank a lot and left early with only photos of the lives of others.

…

Now, without the crowds or cameras, we swam across and set up the low-level Tyrolean traverse, caught a haul of fish, slept well beneath a warm night, to the sound of the sea in its rise and fall.

Tom led the first pitch. I prussiked it as Steve led up to below the off-width overhang. The accompaniment of the sea was ever with us.

I followed Steve, then set off for the overhang, a little unwilling, certain I would not be able to do it. It was easy. Graded just 16 or so, sound rock, knees gripping well in the crack, handholds where they were needed, dolerite smell, salt taste, Tasmania, Tasmania, leading into the restless breeze.

The remaining pitches were much the same grade, even the last pitch which Steve and I insisted Tom should do because it looked hard. Overhung a little, it was just step out on good holds, good rock, good protection, speak to the air, high spirits, fast blood.

Clamber over the boulders at the top—10 years on—and

see the ferns, lichens, grasses, bushes, the same surely. We

abseiled to the big ledge and found the chocks I had

abseiled off 10 years earlier ago now gnawed by salt. The

remains of the fire that had roared in the night were now

mostly gone, the rock around which I had curled to sleep …

unyielding.

So that was 10 years, I thought.

The Candlestick slowly sloughing off the human

interjections, maintaining its immutability, and I, the

traveller in time who placed a shiny chock now half-rotten,

who warmed his hands when these scant coals were fire.

The body now more wrinkled, a little stiffer, less strong—

and the mind changed, changed utterly. The way home

from here another barrier in time to breast. Every thought,

every heartbeat a leap towards death.

10 years were but steps in the total dark, reaching for

fulfilment and finding only further steps in the total dark.

I suppose this year the swell is still the same, and the bush,

and the lichens last another crowded summer on the rock.

Me, only cruel mortality consumes.

...

With apologies to Alfred Lord Tennyson

Climbing story

We almost fell out of the old Hillman. The white gravel of the North Head car park crunched under our feet. Mikl Law and I sat on the gravel in front of the car, leaning back against the steel bumper bar. Reaching back occasionally to scratch smashed bugs off the faded duco. Passing the last of the port bottle. Soaking up the too-early sun.

"Hmm," I grunted.

"Unh."

I clambered back to the car doors, banged the back one open and scrabbled among the old chip papers and nappy wrappers on the back floor. Found the Coke bottle into which Mike had poured the last of the flat Guinness, the flat beer and the red wine from the dregs of the party's glasses and bottles. I wouldn't let him tip in the meths. Back to the bumper bar.

"Unh."

We slurped it down. A strange taste. Then we had none left.

Mikl crawled to the other back door and found some old, cold chips. We nibbled them slowly. It's good to eat after

Lyle Closs impressed by the pollution pouring out of the city -
North Head, Sydney, 1980.   Photo taken by Mikl Law.

drinking. The sun did its work and we stood up after a while and tottered down to the lookout.

"Jeesus." I pointed out beyond South Head. It was a strong pollution day in Sydney—a long, thick brown cloud drew out from the city and its blinking towers and poured over the sea.

"Natural phenomenon," Mikl hardly looked at it.

"World's fucked."

"Plasma of the universe."

"Eh?"

"Thought I should say something."

I nodded. The sea slapped lazily at the great boulders 100 metres below.

…

We hung on the railing and looked down at the tangle of wrecked cars. There was a rough track from the car park to the cliff edge and many weekends there would be a new wreck on the great boulders at the cliff base.

"That Renault's pretty new isn't it," I suggested. It was upside down, smashed almost flat from the impact, wheels sticking out like distraught legs.

"Yep."

"Hmmm."

"What?"

"They have the same size tyres as the Hillman."

"How do you know that?"

"I can't remember."

"Hmmm."

"The tyres look pretty good on that."

"New tyres are expensive!"

"They could be retreads."

"They could be fucked."

"Yeah, but…"

Mikl looked at me and grinned. The dark red hair, the dark eyebrows, wild, eager eyes. Now he was alive. Almost jumping.

"Have you got a wheel wrench?"

"My father-in-law wouldn't let me out without one."

"All right. Let's do it!"

"How'll we get them up here?"

"No problems. Tie them on like a pack. Straight up the fishermen's ladders."

Just east of the North Head lookout, a series of ledges was joined together by rickety wooden ladders and old hemp ropes, white from the salt air. They had been put in place by rock fishermen who clambered down to the sea and were often washed off the rocks during bad weather.

We ransacked the climbing gear for enough slings and rope lengths to tie wheels to our backs, then sauntered down through the low scrub to the notch in the cliff edge and scrambled down the first easy moves to the first ladder.

…

Two of the Renault's tyres were hardly worn and in excellent condition. One of the other two wheels had had its nuts smashed so they were immoveable, and the other tyre had a gash. The wheel wrench fitted the nuts though and we soon had one wheel off and resting on the sea-stained stones. The other was on very tight, but with me holding the wrench near the nut and mike smashing the end with a boulder the tight nuts gave way, and we were two wheels richer.

We messed around with the rope and tapes for a while, then stood and looked at each other, daftly proud of the handiwork.

"Right then." I shifted the clumsy weight, the ropes already cutting into my shoulders. Mikl grinned. We scrambled over the boulders to the ladders. Mikl stopped a minute, looking up to the left, towards the steep walls and overhangs under the lookout.

"Can you see that bolt ladder?"

"Eh?"

"The bolt ladder that leads up to the lookout." He pointed up there.

"Bugger me. D'you know who put that up?" The line of rusty bolts climbed up a clear line, a high, narrow 50 metre corner that stepped left above big overhangs and ended at the lookout railing.

"No idea," he said. "Did you see the bolts at the top."

"I just looked at the wrecks."

"Hmmm." He shifted the wheel on his back and started up. Halfway up the ladders we stopped at a ledge and re-tied the awkward loads. It was hard not to laugh. Tourists were appearing at the lookout and we were part of the morning's entertainment. Another thing to point out to Grandma.

As we climbed over the top a collection of young boys hovered about, asking questions, wanting to be part of the little adventure. Mikl walked ahead, his hands behind his back to help take the weight. I took my wheel off my back and rolled it along. We threw them on the back seat and took a rest. The sun was now well up, the day heating fast.

"You've got some water in the boot haven't you?"

"Oh yeah," I said. "My father-in-law wouldn't let me out without it."

"Let's have a sip."

We sipped the slightly oil-flavoured water from the plastic jerrycan. Sitting on the bonnet, looking at the tourists chattering about the lookout.

"Might as well do some climbing I guess," Mikl said.

"I suppose. What did you have in mind?"

He looked at my slyly, and grinned.

"What about freeing that bolt ladder up to the lookout…?"

And so this is a climbing story.

...

Ian Lewis and Lyle Closs, Lost World, Tasmania, 1972

Third Bird

I am pounding at the keyboard. My fingers flail in the air between words. I am immersed in Astral Weeks. A chaotic jumble of semi-comprehensible prose is battered onto the paper. It is Hobart, it is 1973.

"Fucking come on!" The door bursts open. Ian Lewis wants to climb. I want anything else but. It is chilly, grey. Hobart and autumn glooming. He stands in the doorway of my bare, rented student room, looks at me with amused annoyance, his eyes half closed. "Get your arse out. Come on, it's time we did that fucking line."

I am hardly awake. "Fucking hell mate. It's cold!"

"Fuck it, get your arse out of here. It's not fucking cold." These are our articulate years. He walks in and starts shoving nuts and slings into my old pack. "Christ almighty. Come on."

I moan and push the rickety table aside, start to haul warmer clothes on, pull on my Blundstone elastic-sided boots. Wishing for something else. Something beyond the close walls of Tasmania. I throw my PAs at Ian—he shoves them in after the climbing gear. Jeff Burgess grins from the door.

"You want to climb! Get out of the fucking car!" Lew abused us. We clambered out of Jeff's dad's old FB Holden. The salmon pink car had been painted using a vacuum cleaner spray paint attachment. When his dad installed modern nylon seatbelts, Jeff scrounged the old home-made leather seatbelts and turned them into leather gear belts.

We slouched up the dirt and boulder track behind Ian, up to the walking track under the Organ Pipes. Hands shoved into pockets against the cold breeze. The herb-like smell that comes from I know not which plant, but which feels like a place in my mind, clung to my senses. The re-growth still struggled five years after the bestial bushfires of '67 when the sky had turned to Hades and the mountain's green paradise had turned to skeletal shapes and blistered rock.

There was, as usual, no-one else on the cliff. We stopped on the track to admire the unclimbed line. A narrow spear of shadow—100 metres straight up. It's cold, so the leader's hands are warmed by the adrenalin of the sharp end, but the second's hands suck cold from the stone, the mind less engaged because of the security of the rope above.

I led the first pitch, up and around the small overhang. Ian led the second, up the clean crack to a small ledge below the over-hanging off-width. Below us, enjoyable climbing. Not enough to test fear. I struggled up into the off-width. It pushed me out when I want to go up. There was a jug on the lip, but it led nowhere. I struggled back down, grunting, annoyed. Ian took the rope from me, and was soon immersed in the crack, a powerhouse of determination.

I shivered on the belay. Somewhere below Jeff sat on a rock, watching. Somehow Ian ground up and through the off-width, and soon grinned from the ledge above. I shuddered and headed into the rock again, but at the off-width my hands had become clubs and I made the mistake of grabbing the hold outside the crack, couldn't get back in and I was swinging in space. Grabbed the rock, hauled, Ian hauled, grunted and stood on holds again, fingers in armpits. Half unfrozen, I climbed up to the belay, then fingers in armpits again and I growled and yelped as the blood jerked back into my fingers' veins.

The air seemed warmer as I led above Lew, on small holds, almost face climbing. A hand hold broke and I swung briefly from the jammed knuckle of the little finger of my left hand. Exhiliration swamped me as the sun half-shone through the clouds and made the weathered dolerite a warn orange. The stone's surface that fabulous dolerite friction that needs no chalk. Out on the face of the world with moves hard enough to work the mind and the muscles to a slow lilt of careful movement that takes the spirit closer to the soul.

I belayed in warmer air at the top of the climb. Leaned over to watch Ian climb up. His slow grin saying how much he was enjoying the climb, the day. Two crows skimmed by the crag lower down. "Hey Lew—two black birds." He looked out at them and nodded. "Three black birds is bad luck isn't it?" I called down. He shrugged.

Seconds later a third crow sailed effortlessly past us. "Hey Lew!" He looked up. I pointed out at the gliding bird. "Third bird!" He shook his head and returned to the grace and ease of the pitch, a delicious comparison to the grunt of the overhang below. Such a time we had. Such a day, before our separate times of madness. A climb's perfection clawed and clasped from cold Tasmanian days. So many days, and so few.

...

On such days the rock is warm or the nevé firm, and the air hints of something beyond. Something almost reached. Almost.

...

Third Bird, a classic grade 17 route on the Organ Pipes outside Hobart, Tasmania was first climbed by Ian Lewis and Lyle Closs in 1973.

Peter Kuestler at 6500m on K2's North Ridge, 1990

Instinct

I am wallowing in stone. Tom Williams has led the first pitch, and I've floundered up, still not acknowledging that I have no desire for the struggle. The life I am leading does not point me with any compulsion towards steeper walls, smaller holds.

I am still breathing hard on the belay holds. I lean back on my harness, letting the bolt take the weight. Tom is slowly grinding upwards above me, grunting now and then. I'm seeing a day ahead of me with few highlights. A long belay, then being hauled up this long, hard pitch. Boiling a billy of tea later though, that will be good. I resist the urge to pick my nails. I look down the at the jagged boulder field 20 metres below, unusual under a Blue Mountains crag. I drop a gob of spit. It lands three metres out from the base of the wall

A couple of hours later I tie a figure-of-eight knot in the end of the old pink 11mm rope and throw it off the sandstone cliff-top. Hold onto the rope to lean out and look down, check there are no snags. The rope flips and sways in the warm Blue Mountains air. Free of the cliff all the way. The end is maybe three metres out from the wall near the belay. Should be easy enough to swing into the belay bolts and from there abseil to the deck. I clip in the figure-of-eight descender, shift the rucksack on my shoulders. 'We'll do an easier one next,' Tom grins. His fingers are dry, white from chalk. ' I need to live next to a gym,' I grunt. 'And I hate abseiling.'

Step over the edge, careful to put the rope into the small depression on the cliff edge so it hangs in the right place.

I shuffle the rope up into the descender for a few feet until it starts to slide more easily. Look up and see Tom peering over the edge. Let the rope slide through my right hand, pulling it behind my thigh to slow the descent as the weight of the rope below me becomes less. My left fingers rest gently against the taut rope above me as I glide down, spinning slowly. I can see the footholds and handholds of the belay now and I slide more slowly, watching for the best time to stop and swing into the belay. As I glance down at the boulders on the ground, the knot at the end of the rope nudges up against my right fist.

I am swinging in space, too far out from the cliff. Holding the knot at the end of the rope against my thigh, swinging back and forth, trying to get in to the rock and grab the hand holds at the belay. Twisting round in space, finding it hard, with no purchase on anything but air, to swing the right way.

There isn't enough rope left to twist round my leg to free up both hands. My left hand flails aimlessly. My weight drags the descender down the rope, trying to slide onto the knot. That's what the knot is there for, I think. So let the knot jam and hold me while I swing. I lower myself the last inches and the knot squirms up against the figure-of-eight. Jammed as solid as rock. Now it's easier to swing, and I start to get a useful motion into my dead weight. My right hand leads the swing, the left rests easy on the rope, just there for balance...then the knot pops through the descender...

...

I am plodding up a 55-degree ice slope 2000 metres above the glacier on K2's North Ridge in a place with no mercy. I had let the expedition cook, Fidar, get away with an extra hour in bed. 'Can't let the tail wag the dog,' Steve Swenson would say later. Yeah.

I have to get the load from base camp at 5500m to Camp 2 at 7500m, and the sun is warming the steep white fields. I should be slogging upwards on firm nevé with a steady three breaths for each upward plod. But it's later in the day than it should be.

The surface is collapsing in slush under my crampons. I am wallowing in hoarse gasps between the icy mush and a blinding sun. Totally dependent on the fixed ropes. Driving my body to something incomprehensible.

'You go to summit?' the Sherpas from the Japanese expedition had asked. 'No,' I said. They looked confused. A white guy—he should at least want to go to the summit. I touched my chest and said 'Australian sherpa.' They fell about laughing.

Peter Kuestler and I had left advance base camp in the first light of day. When we unpacked at the start of the climbing, Peter realized he had left his descender behind, and raced off alone back through the crevasse field to the camp to pick it up. I haven't seen him for a long time. The first 1000m to Camp 1 was relatively easy. Steps already there, plugged by Steve, Greg Child, Greg Mortimer and Phil Ershler the day before as they headed up to set up Camp 3. My load is needed to re-stock Camp 2 for their future summit attempt.

At high altitude it's often useful to have a second brain nearby. A couple of weeks earlier I had raced down the fixed ropes from Camp 2 to Camp 1 as the day closed down. It was getting darker and darker, and harder and harder to safely change over from rope to rope at each of the ice screw belays on the face. Four abseils from Camp 1, without a torch, and worried I might screw up a changeover in the dark, I had brushed my face and realized I still had my dark glasses on.

My water bottle is now empty. I am wishing Camp 2 was closer. I am a little light-headed, but the only thing to do is to plug on. The pack feels monstrous, and occasionally, when I lose my footing, pulls me backwards. I reach another ice-screw point. The screw has disappeared into the face as the thaw of each day and freeze of each night has built up the layers of ice. I jerk the ropes out of the ice as much as they'll come. I unclip the Jumar from the lower rope, clip it into the top rope, then begin again to step and Jumar.

I ram the crampons into the face to get the deepest purchase, hoping the damned surface will hold. Steps collapse under me time and time again, usually just as I have begun to establish a rhythm. It's so draining. My feet are sore from being wrenched inside the hard plastic boots. I feel like an old fighter slugging out a bad fight, desperate for the final bell. I slug up to the next ice screw. The pack's uncomfortable. I shrug it to get a better fit. Unclip the top belay sling.

A footstep feels awkward, so I shuffle on the footholds. Forget to clip the sling back on above the ice screw. I only have the Jumar connected now, but that hasn't registered. Kick the crampon in hard. Shift the foot to get the heel taking weight better. I unclip the Jumar, shift my weight…the pack flops back, tugging me off balance…as I tip back I remember that I forgot to clip the top loop, that I am two thousand metres above the ground …

…

The knot bursts out of the descender and I fall off the end of the rope…

Instinctively the muscles of my left hand clamp tight as I fall. The knot slams into my left fist, the rope stretches… and I stop…

"FUCK!"

I swing, dangling below the end of the rope, holding only by the strength of my left hand. Two metres out from the face. Twenty metres above the boulders. Tom watches helplessly, wide-eyed with distant fear. I swing myself towards the rock once, twice, and finally grasp a small hold with my right fingers. My feet flap for a second, then gratefully rest on good footholds, but the wall is steep and totally without protection.

Between me and the belay bolts, two metres above, are two serious moves I needed to be hauled up a few hours back. I cannot move from these holds. The rope, at full stretch, is now pulling me up and out, away from the holds. I let it go. It springs upwards into the air, far beyond reach. Now the weight of the pack and the steepness of the wall combine to keep me just off balance. Without a moment's concern, I take off the pack and drop it and the gear it contains to the ground. I hear the nasty thump as it smashes into the rocks.

Now I am very alone.

50 metres above, Tom races to join our ropes and soon abseils down to close above me, swinging into the bolts. The ends of the ropes are tied directly to his harness.

'Fuckin' hell Lyle!' he yells.

'Fuckin' hell,' I can only agree.

…

I tip backwards off K2's ice wall. Instinctively, my right hand flies out. The tips of my fingers catch the drooping rope and for a moment I pause there, the fingers closing like a slow vice. I pull myself back to the vertical. With my left hand, I grab the karabiner on my belay loop and clip it to the rope. Then I start shivering violently.

I grab the Jumar and shakily clip that in too, then lean carefully back and let the rope take my weight. I shut my eyes and breathe a few quiet breaths. Then look down the face. At the huge avalanche debris fan that destroyed the Japanese advance base. At the minute dots that are the camp's remains.

Down to my left, the ropes lead back down and across to the point of rock, then drop straight down to Camp 1, hidden behind bulges in the face. Peter Kuestler is back there somewhere. What is it like to see a companion fall so far, tumbling and smashing, to his death? But this is no place for reflection.

Instinctively, I push the Jumar up the rope and pitch a crampon into the face, step upwards, and again, and again, and again.

…

My good friends Don Holmes and Peter Reynolds died, respectively of cancer and a 20m ground-fall. Karl Prinz, the indestructible two-metre-tall, 100-kilogram German with whom I made the first ascents of Carlyle and the Wild

West Route on Federation Peak died in a taxi accident in Perth, Western Australia. Richard Schmidt, whose home-made beer and popcorn Ian Lewis, Bob McMahon and I had enjoyed one drunken night in Launceston, died in an avalanche on Annapurna III.

...

The distance between this hard, warm flesh and the end of all time is but a moment's instinct, something as tangible as a glimpse through curtains of an emotion walking by. I am alive today and not rotten and soughing off my bones into a dank, black earth.

The phantasms of our dreams, the masks of tragedy and comedy, sit round the campfire with us and wait their moment, then curse and cackle when they realise they have missed their moment by the thickness of a shadow on a wall, of an instinctive muscular spasm within the inordinate fractions of time.

...

*Jeff Burgess and Bryan Kennedy slothing at the campsite
below the summit of Mt Oakley, Tasmania, 1974*

Sloth

I sit at the base of the Roaches in Derbyshire, Whillans' ghost still clinging to the Sloth overhang. A grunt. It's me standing up, not someone jamming the void. And I'm looking out, not up. Looking back.

Past the Whillans Hut, past those expeditions, down past Peter Jackson writing to me in Sydney to say that Whillans had died, back further to Tasmania, 1968, grainy black-and-whites of 50s English climbers. An envious boy's finger touches the mirage—climbs burnished with impossibility and distance. Somewhere half a planet away, beyond the confines of a small island.

...

I led my first Severe (15) at the Organ Pipes in 1969. Someone took pics with my camera. At home, I opened the camera's back, wound the film carefully back into the cartridge. Picked up the film a few days later at the chemist in North Hobart. Every print black. My first climbs burnt. Stupid boy.

Bryan Kennedy, Jeff Burgess and I ploughed through the Tasmanian rain forest in 1973, canvas H frame packs heavy with climbing gear, leather straps grinding into sore shoulders.

The ridge on Mt Oakley had never been climbed. The long, jagged outline of dolerite had titillated me for a few years, peaking out of bushwalkers' slides. Half-jolly people in thick leather boots, green army-surplus trousers and checked woollen shirts. Clumsy A-frame rucksacks and japara parkas waterproofed with linseed oil and terrapin.

They stood smiling, half-obscuring the sweep of the ridge soaring down to the valley below the plateau summit. They were the passing generation of Tasmanian bushwalkers who still found places no-one had ever been. Mainstays of the Hobart Walking Club. Some had walked in earnest file to the summit of Oakley. They looked at the splendid views from the plateau edge and walked back to FJ Holdens, Humber Hawks, side-valve Dodge vans.

They plucked leeches from their ankles. They boiled billies and warned youngsters about the dangers of hypothermia in Tasmania's changeable mountain winds. Their heroes were Jack Thwaites and Leo Luckman, who had fought for the summit of Federation Peak, but were beaten by upstart mainlanders.

The Oakley ridge is about 350 m high, but long and jagged. The fabulous columnar dolerite of so many Tasmanian mountains and sea cliffs. Jutting out from a plateau that rises to a small peak where the ridge meets the mountain mass.

We camped on alpine grasses among low mountain scoparia and stunted King Billy pines as the clouds slowly descended. Listened through the night to the delicious patter of light rain on canvas. The old Paddy Pallin single-skin three-man tent—green canvas, door flaps that tied shut with cotton tape, no floor, no poles. Best for two people really. We plucked up the sides of the orange plastic groundsheet occasionally to make sure it didn't flip outside and let water in.

Careful not to touch the tent roof. If you touched the canvas, you had to run a finger from that point to the base of the roof slope so the drips would run down the trail and trickle down the tent wall rather than drip on your face.

We spent the next day either in the tent or standing in the drizzle among the mists—in our woollen army trousers, checked shirts and japara cotton parkas. Bryan in his white ski jumper and woollen beanie. Jeff's long flaming hair flicking about in the chill breezes. Wafting a plate up and down by the coals to keep the struggling fire alive. Holding tea mugs in our hands to keep them warm. Hoping the weather would clear. We only had a few spare days.

Towards evening the clouds lifted. A warmer breeze brushed the damp air. We sat outside, light conversation among friends. Drinking hot chocolate. Seeing how far we could lower chocolate-thickened spit and still suck it back.

We woke in the morning to a clouded sky. There were suggestions of rain in the distance, but after a lazy discussion, Bryan and I pulled the climbing gear together.

Ewbank crackers (nuts)—some on tape slings, some on laid rope. A couple of prized Moac chockstones, peg hammers, rope-slings and tape-slings, steel karabiners, Chouinard pegs and some lovely new, thin Hi-Tens angle pegs. Two inch nylon tape waistbands. My leather-trimmed PAs, Bryan's tattered JPs with the rock-hard soles. I took the day pack, Bryan our 11mm white nylon laid rope. Jeff stood below the summit with us as we looked west at the grey clouds, out where the weather comes from.

"What are those clouds doing?" Bryan asked.

"Buggered if I know, but I wish they'd go away," I grunted.

Jeff just screwed his eyes up and looked.

"Might as well, I guess," I said.

"Yep," Bryan shrugged. "Keep the fire going," he grinned at Jeff.

We slipped and shuffled down the long gully. Our legs were quickly soaked with water off the low richea and mountain pepper bushes, our backsides wet from sliding on pineapple grass. Every few minutes we would stop and look west. The grey clouds had shifted to distant rain squalls, the morning light shining cloud-white among the rain.

I led the first, easy pitch nervously, looking at the weather. Bridging, jugs, that worn dolerite surface that clings to the skin. The faint smell of Jurassic stone.

Worrying about climbing in rain, or more seriously, being caught on the cliff in some serious Tasmanian mountain weather. We yelled back and forth. Bryan followed quickly, and we stood on a ledge, looking up at the chimney and crack line spearing up to the first spike on the ridge. Grey dolerite on the inside walls, weathered brown on the outward facing faces. Looming, serious.

It was definitely going to rain. We could see the squalls approaching, maybe a storm. Hell, life was very long ahead of us and the cliff would always be there. There was no competition with other climbers—not with ourselves, not with a looming future. We wanted sunny rock, easy days, something like when we climbed Tornado Ridge on Stacks Bluff, when the sun shone all day despite the high winds and we laughed and yahooed the long ridge day to a grand conclusion.

This day though loomed drear. Hard, wet, grunt-ugly climbing inside mountain downpours. Having to classical abseil down sodden ropes with frozen fingers.

We abseiled the pitch and trudged back up the gully to the summit and the tent, waiting for the rain. Waiting for proof we had done the right thing, but not really worried if it didn't. There was plenty of time.

The rain didn't come. Maybe one short cloud-pushed drizzle, then the day stayed dry. We drank more tea, more hot chocolate, expecting squalls. The time drizzled by and we slept, half-annoyed, half relieved. We left the next morning without going back to look again at the prize passed by. Another day, any day soon now, and we'd be back, and the sun would shine...

I don't know why we never went back. I heard some years later that someone had climbed it, and it didn't mean anything much to me then. It annoys me now though. It could easily have been ours, but we made weak excuses and walked away. How could I have been so stupid? Why didn't I hammer up the line and to hell with the weather? Why did I think life was long? The ridge was too easily passed by.

...

I am annoyed too that I am not now, here at The Roaches, seethingly angry with myself. I dreamed it, and I gave up without trying. I should be angry. I should be paying myself back for that failure, for too many failures, by slamming fists into The Sloth, re-awakening the ability, re-creating the old photo-charged dreams.

But here I am walking along under the wintry crags, on the soil Whillans trod, looking for an easy way out, a Hard Severe to justify the day. I've already begged off the HVS Greg Mortimer has led. There's a smell of wood smoke among the trees.

Life has too easily passed by. Too many climbs burnt. Stupid, stupid boy.

...

The first people ever to ski on the Man o' War Glacier,
North Victoria Land, Antarctica, 1988

The last expedition

Giles Kershaw was flying jumbos for British Airways.
Making a living so he could fly to Antarctica in the summer
months.

We had a pizza and coffee down the street from the
Holiday Inn in central Sydney. Talked about polar history.
He told me about his flight across Antarctica with Dick
Smith. I told him what Greg Mortimer and I were planning.

To sail around 5000 kilometres south to the Ross Sea in a
chartered 20 metre fishing boat. To ski 120 km inland to Mt
Minto and make the first ascent of the 4163-metre peak.
But what if it all fell apart? What if the boat was crushed in
ice and sank? Could Giles fly in and get us out?

"I'm sorry Lyle. If something happens to you in North
Victoria Land we just can't get to you. We can fly to
McMurdo Sound, but Victoria Land is too far. The
Americans won't sell us fuel, and getting enough fuel from
Chile to McMurdo Sound to enable us to fly to North
Victoria Land and all the way back, well, maybe if you had
a million?"

He grinned. "What about flying direct from Australia?" I
asked. He shook his head. "It's just too far. You have to be

able to carry enough fuel to fly back, and only the biggest planes can do that. Only governments can afford Hercules, let alone ski-equipped Hercules."

...

It was 1987. Giles had vast experience of flying in Antarctica for the British Antarctic Survey and had pioneered the first private expeditions into Antarctica. He said with a modest smile that he knew most of the ice runways in Antarctica, and where most of the fuel caches were. It was a great loss when he died just a few years later, his gyrocopter flicked by the whim of a gust into a mountainside on remote Blaiklock Island.

...

We sailed south in January 1988 knowing that only the US Coast Guard could save us if the ice decided to crush the boat. Or maybe the Greenpeace ship which was sailing a different agenda in the region.

When the little craft became trapped in the ice outside the Ross Sea, the Coast Guard icebreaker spoke to us only grudgingly—we might have interrupted their schedule with our annoying private expedition problems. The ice floated apart a day later when the wind changed, and we sailed into the Ross Sea. The cliffs of Cape Adare looked small from where we sailed, a few miles out from the shore, but are 2,500 metres high. The icebergs were golden in the late-night light. The sun set behind an iceberg with a glint of green, then rose again into our early morning.

...

Greg slammed the skidoo up the steep ice slopes and over open crevasses, smashing one of the sledges, but ensuring we made it over Football Saddle the third night, ready for the long haul up the Tucker Glacier towards the lower slopes of Mt Minto.

Jonathan Chester and Chris Hilton then took the unloaded skidoo back to the boat for more fuel, but the sea ice broke up and the skidoo floated away in the night. So we man-hauled for four days, left everything we could at an advance camp, climbed the mountain, and came back to the camp two days later. We radioed the boat.

"I have asked the Greenpeace boat to stay here until you get back," Don Richards told us. "Their helicopter is ready to airlift you off the glacier. I can't allow us to be the last boat to leave the Ross Sea."

...

It was about then that the filament that was adventure began to unravel. In retrospect, Giles' few private flights into Antarctica, however expensive at that time, were a hint that everything was soon to change. Our small boat expedition, an adventure of the world that was, began to be overwhelmed by the world that now is.

...

The weather was foul for three days and we hauled the sledges back towards the sea, six men racing against small time and small food and fuel, towards four men and a woman on a small craft that was our lifeline. But then, two days hauling distance from the coast, the weather cleared, and we were told that the helicopter would be with us within half an hour. And the world ground to an ugly halt, and our dreams of self-reliance became muddied and clumsy.

The chopper could only take two people at a time. Two, then two more. For half an hour Greg and I were in a silent, exquisite world of our own. I wished that the weather would turn bad, that the chopper couldn't return and we'd have to haul the last sledge the 48 kilometres to the sea in one desperate surge, clamber on board the small boat against freezing waves, and sail north among the bergs, desperate to miss the first winter storms.

That we would do it without the help of big boats and helicopters, satellite communications and serious icebreakers.

Greg walked away from the tent, out onto the 30 km wide Tucker Glacier. I didn't realise then, didn't realise until much later, that he was mourning a great loss. Before us, a great emptiness had opened up. The world of expeditions travelling to places where the world could not help them had gone forever.

Selfishly, we were annoyed and sad that the silence was about to fade. That the isolation which could have tested and proved our small human reserves was about to be taken from us by the whoomp, whoomp, whoomp of an infernal machine. An infernal loss.

...

People who once made reputations by real exertions now maintain sponsor-driven lives by doing ever more strained variations on tired themes. Multiple ascents of multiple mountains. Multiple marathons on multiple continents. And little lies creep in to justify the sponsorship. That Antarctica has been crossed when people were actually airlifted off hundreds of miles from the sea. That the situation was life-threatening when there was a plane ready to lift them off the icefloe at any time.

Giles Kershaw's company can fly you, or Greg Mortimer's company can cruise you to Antarctica and back in the space of an annual holiday. Selling the pretence of a world now gone.

...

Memory

If I pluck from a distant branch of the tree of my mind a fervent moment and then watch where that moment leads… It is 1970. I am 17, sitting in the Tasmanian Library in Hobart, struggling to study, wanting to be elsewhere. They stride among the tables, grinning, cocky, swaggering. Black japara parkas say they are outdoor types. One black haired, expressive, outgoing, bounding. The other more tightly sprung, slightly shorter, a mass of fair hair. Both with a wildness, an enthusiasm that sets them apart. Gods of the air that surrounds them. I want to be with them, to soak up a greater sense than the dull flush of a Hobart winter. A sense that life has more.

...

I am walking towards the hidden cliffs of Clifton in Tasmania. Sheep-cropped fields, dots of sheep shit shiny from the morning dew. Blue skies. Ahead of me walk Peter Jackson, Bob Bull, John Moore. Gods of a Victorian climbing dawn. I am just a clumsy boy yet walk in these footsteps.

...

Lyle Closs, three days from the road, DuCane Range,
Tasmania, 1975. Photo taken by Bob McMahon.

The big old Ford is full of people. Bob and Angela Bull and their young son. John Moore and a girlfriend. Me and Don Holmes. Drumming along dirt roads looking for a crag that might or might not exist. On the map the hillside looks craggy, but no-one has actually seen a cliff. Tanara Walls was it called? Stopping among a eucalyptus forest for children to pee by the roadside, a tape copied off one of Bob's bootleg Dylan albums blaring from my portable tape player. Not finding any kind of cliff. Trying to smoke one of Bob's Senior Service fags, and coughing half to die after just a few drags.

...

Dropping into the Bull house in Collinsvale under another wet Tasmanian day, watching the local kids drive their body-less car up the road. Bob saying he'd have to move further into the mountains some day because the Hobart yuppies were moving in and driving out the locals. He wasn't yet accepted as a local though as he'd only lived there 10 years.

...

Hammering the VW up the fire track, as hard as possible up the steep section, usually needing a few tries, but worth the effort to save the three mile walk to Sunshine Possibilities, the warm crag out the back of Mt Wellington. It's illegal, but someone we know has the key to the gate at the start of the track

...

Going to see Bob McMahon, the dark haired one from the library, in his Lenah Valley flat. The green legged steel frame chairs. Suzie pregnant with Andreas, her jeans unzipped under her jumper.

...

Drinking into the night with McMahon and Bob Bull, then lurching into Bob's battered old black Beetle and heading up the fire track. The VW getting stuck halfway up the steep section. Sitting on the dirt piled beside the road and finishing the beer. Clouds skimming by the moon, a deep black sky and bright stars, bright stars.

...

Trying with Ian Lewis and Mungrl to get to Sunshine Possibilities by a different route, from the fire track off the big bend on Mt Wellington, in Ian's Ford Anglia. Getting stuck at a hill and using an old climbing rope to try to haul the damn thing up. But that's a different branch of memory's tree, with just some similar images.

...

Driving to Launceston with Ian after doing a couple of routes at The Pavilion, sleeping on McMahon's floor just a few days after Oscar Paniza the puppy had died in the street, ants eating out his eyes. Suzy pregnant with Iseult. Drinking Richard Schmidt's home brew and eating his popcorn then spewing it all out McMahon's side window.

...

Talking with McMahon to the large men who owned the bulldozer and graders we had just been trying to start out the back of Ben Lomond. McMahon luckily knowing one of their cousins, sweetening the air that had threatened to grow very thick and nasty.

...

Walking the DuCane Range with McMahon, with his friend Kathy as a limp appendage to the flourishing joy of the high mountain cold. Van Morrison's Astral Weeks on that old tape player among the stunted trees and tarns of the Labyrinth and the bottle of Galliano. Downing the Guinness standing in a snowstorm under Falling Mountain, Kathy shivering alone in the tent. In the DuCane Hut, turning on Hendrix and getting stuck into the cask of red wine, putting on lipstick to disturb the bushwalkers.

...

Watching John Moore glide across the middle overhang on Carnap at Clifton. A monstrous climbing ability little used. Jackson followed, then Bull, then I, untutored in jamming, pinged off under the overhang, and swung in space three metres below the next hold. Hand-over-handed up the rope to the small ledge. Complimented for this. Walking back over the green fields feeling close to the sky.

...

Bare feet on the damp gravely sands of a Coles Bay morning. Stretching the morning tensions out of the body in that squatting, every-muscle-tensing action that sometimes comes over me. Peter Jackson imitating my every move, straight-faced.

Listening to the mythology I missed, of the first ascent of Incipience. Of winds whipping at them on obscenely thin artificial climbing on Coles Bay's thick-grained granite in years past. Yet I am here, subsumed for a weekend into an iconoclastic Iliad. Following Mike McHugh, the blonde one from the library, up the crux of Rh Negative, great splashes of his blood on the crack and the walls after granite grains the size of peas had peeled off the back of his fist.

...

And things drift away. London, Bath, Ballarat, Exeter. I write florid essays of hope and loss to Jackson for decades, until, not knowing why, words start to dry up. An older boy's grip on his barely grasped past starts to loosen, to fail. So action fades to memory, and the wild emotion of young gods fades to mythology, loosely defined. Defined more loosely with each dribbling day.

As if that is life.

...

Ian Lewis, Peter (Mungrl) Reynolds, Don Holmes, Lyle Closs,
Jeff (Red) Burgess - Lowdina, Tasmania, 1971

Glass

It seems that the events of the 35 years since I started climbing comprise a vastness barely less than eternity; and at the same time a flash of light, incomprehensible in the speed of its passing.

I started there. A clumsy, enthusiastic boy blathering up climbs others had thought too hard, wondering what the fuss was about, loving the physical, enjoying the praise, wanting more, always wanting more. I was the colt running in the field, just running. Just climbing.

I have arrived here. The thing that is here is barely here. It is just a knowledge, a whisper. Something half-remembered, half-forgotten. Something like a glass splinter found under the skin, not felt, just found with some surprise and prised out by old fingers, rusty blades.

Our party trick was for Mungrl to stub out his cigarettes on the soles of my feet. I walked barefoot for a winter and more on Hobart's cold streets. My soles were so thick that I soloed Morfydd barefoot between bouts of heavy drinking at Arapiles, the same trip on which I hurled a burning log at Ben Maddison's forehead.

Small slivers of glass used to glide from city streets into my thick callused soles and slowly work their way up until they found nerves deep under the surface and I would finally feel the pain. I would dig into the horny skin until I had found the tiny piece of glass and prise it out on the end of a heavy needle. Mungrl liked to dig them out at parties with his penknife while people winced and complained.

Some I couldn't find. They annoyed me for a while then the pain went away. I have tried to find them, but they seem to have gone in too far, to have slipped past the nerves unseen, unfelt. Or maybe they slipped under my skin in other ways. Perhaps at the Hobart party when anxieties overwhelmed my fingers and the glass exploded in my hand. Maybe at the old house in North Hobart when I punched the window in. They show up in X-rays now, shard shadows. Anomalies, the radiologists mutter. Bloody anomalies.

Mungrl should have been a Warrane lout, but at high school he had a fight with someone in the wrong crowd and they stopped talking to him. He had no-one to play with, and so fell in with schoolwork. Against the odds, he passed his School Certificate and left behind all those who had rejected him. At Matric he fell in with climbers. Mungrl. It was his choice of spelling. Peter Reynolds was the name his mother preferred.

He was a good friend, without pretensions or prejudices. My memories of him are brief flashes of light. Swimming at Lake Valhalla when Ian Lewis and I climbed the first two zooming lines of the Trinity on Stacks Bluff. I have a poor photo of him grinning naked from the water. A party in Melbourne where he lived briefly with me and Jonathan Wurth, when we were trying to get the band to work. The Rolling Stones' Midnight Rambler always reminds me of that night. Another day, when the local electrician showed us why the guitars were giving us little shocks—one touch on a pipe or radiator and we would have been fried. His story of running through the streets of Collingwood with Jonathan, five hoods hard behind, chasing them for the wad Jonathan had absent-mindedly flashed at the local pub. Smashing beer bottles on the train line below Lowdina after a lousy day's climbing, Jeff Burgess looking on in puzzled dismay. Ken McConnell helpless with laughter trying to repeat a Mungrl joke about someone's lousy runner placements. Spending a weekend in bed with his girlfriend, because they felt like it. Messing round on the salt-gritty sea-polished red granite of White Water Wall. Telling us tales from the New Norfolk mental hospital where he worked as an orderly.

He helped me and Jonathan fix the replacement window at the house at Malvern, in south-east Melbourne. After we moved to Collingwood the badly fitted glass was blown out of the frame by a storm and shattered on the head of a child. The little girl was unhurt, not even scratched, merciful God.

We went different ways. He joined the army and some years later was getting back into climbing in Queensland. Placed a runner half-way up an easy 35m route at Kangaroo Point. A hold broke near the top and he fell to the ground and was gone. Merciless God.

There is a grave somewhere and I guess it would be in Tasmania. I hope his parents brought him back. There is good granite in Tasmania. It buffs up into a dull reddish pink, irreducible over centuries. The polish on his gravestone should be almost a mirror. His old body a weathered shard of life. An anomaly. Shifting round within my flesh like old glass.

...

Greg Mortimer near the end of
Red Rocks Ridge, Greenland, 2006

If there was a yesterday it is this instant

There is a scream. It rises slowly in the craw, gagging and choking before it reaches the air, sagging grudgingly back into the sluggish dread from which it tried to emerge. It is my desire, my long and crusty desire to fly.

Free from burdens, free from anguish, free and sleep-like from damnation and pressure and other people's god-damned excesses of annoyance, of frustration and despair. It is my own little pocketbook of desperation slammed shut inside the gorge, but wanting, ever and often wanting, to scream.

So there I am on the crumbling ledge. It's conglomerate and my friends are cackling. Gobs of stone drop off almost before sweaty fingerprints have exchanged the scum of finger-pads for the stone's dusty surface. Plunging past Ben's head. Greg's grin above and whoop-whoop of delight at the endless outrageousness of the long, high and rotten Red Rocks Ridge.

Greenland swoops and is endless about us—vast fjords, awesome snowfields and staggering cascades of ice, a grand vizier's sweep of sea lit gladly by glimmering icebergs from unseen distant calving places, shimmer of passing whales, hammer-blows of rock walls and ridges searing down thousands of metres into the fjord-black and arctic-char-chilled depths.

Three colourful dots pitted meaninglessly among the blathering distances of nobodies.

Mutter, hammer, clip and call. Rope and step and rope and shudder. Pitch and blackness, belay and butterflies scarring stomach walls. Pitch and the blink of long, long daylight. The hum of silence. The caw of black birds. A fly nonsensically lost.

Waiting for our plateau-babbling future, musk ox implacably resting among blueberries, weird fungi and far, far distances. Untrammelled, untravelled, untrodden.

We glimmer like painted icebergs on the red, red, rotten rock.

They leave me in the middle, and lead laughing and chattering. "You're gonna love this" shudders in through my implacable fears and determined ambition to never ever climb again in this damned, dim life. "You're gonna love this," Ben cackles.

Pitch and pitch and summery, blubbering pitch. Long swathes of slobby rock without protection, then a hex among pebbles, a cam in a crumbling crack. There was one though. One. One Moac chockstone, blessed of a generation, that slotted and ground powerfully into hard rock. Leave me here. Tie me off. Don't make me climb on among this confusion between desert and cliff. Dusty, brittle, nervous, emotionally unstable. Me. The ridge. Out there the unswept stable of massive walls and ridges, power gullies and dive-bombing gulch heads. Blooming red waves of crumbling geology.

Do I quiver? Do I blanch? Am I clay and therefore more than this shoddy pretence of a cliff-scape?

Long, long the pitches when we untie the belay and start climbing to allow the leader to find the next belay. Ten pitches and we reach a sand-sloughing left-leading shelf, up to a filthy, shattered chimney. Self-abuse its only likely peroration this side of destiny.

I hide out to the side. Ben hides in the back. Greg crumbles upwards and over the teetering walls and stones. Filth pours in little streams, the ridge's angry sputum.

Ben follows, hauls sacks unwanted in the cramped confines. I grumble, chimney-speak my way up, then the channel, then the blinding summit, the first top-out, the sagging back end of which we have feared for hours. Having seen other ridges drop off the back in massive vertical shears. Blessed be the black vexatious gods though, the top peters down to a ridge that leads on and up and on to the far plateau edge. Far to go.

We chomp salami and smelly cheese. Sip water and thanks. Bless the imblessed implausibility of the conception and imagination that the damn thing could have been a route in the first place. Not me. Oh no not me. Me just fear and a wholesome / unwholesome desire to run away through every second of the fluttering day.

I plunge off the summit on jagged blunderings. Belay on nothing where there is nothing to belay from. Ben and Greg follow protected by the rope leading over a bulge above me. Ben whistles Dixie along the ridge and upwards. Chattering to a listener not with us. We begin to blather, following along the ridge to belays on rocking boulders. The rotten ridge the runner. Hoping not to have to jump off one side if one of us falls off the other, to Jumar back up from the scything depths?

Little summits, little desperadoes. Then bang. The ridge ends at 18 pitches and we are human.

Stumbling, blinking as if the light had just started to shine. Fists pummelling backs with disbelief that such a thing could be. That such a sun might shine and let, through the cracks of the long hot day's light, a shaft of another light.

Another hymn-like memory that chatters still, and yet was fair. That matters much…for the outrageous passing of the day, for the razor through the paper, the whale's breath captured, the arctic hare's confusion, the banged-up ankle, the second massive effort to get the zodiac below the tide line, and the dimming light that crowned us silly little men who went out one day to climb.

...

The next three pieces were written in 2008 after communicating with Bob McMahon and Gerry Narkowicz about the history of Ben Lomond climbing for their new guide. The three soaring 200m lines of The Trinity at Stacks Bluff, Tasmania were climbed over three days in 1972 by Ian Lewis, Lyle Closs and Bryan Kennedy.

Lyle Closs (twice), first ascent, Blue Eyed Sun, Stacks Bluff, Tasmania, 1972

Photos taken by Peter (Mungrl) Reynolds.

And if we fall slowly is there more time left to us?

The Trinity - Blue Eyed Sun

If you take a long fall, your senses grab hold of everything and stuff them glibly, aggressively, into the grab bag that is your brain. They attempt to turn what you thought was an almost endless, long and slow parade of days into a sudden, brilliant urgency because you might not feel the absorbing tug of the rope, because this may be the end and you must garner as much as you can. Then the rope's sensual grasp slows you, holds you and lets you live again. Then those instants replay, and you see the glinting granite crystal as you passed, the mite on the grass stem, the gecko hidden in the crack.

The return to your misjudged sense that the end of your life is an eternity away is mitigated by the realisation that time now passes a little faster, that an end may be imagined, and that it is nearer than it was.

...

We will never know the perceptions of the last Tasmanians who had lived a tribal lifestyle as they bore the depredations, desecrations, of our predecessors and dropped uncontrollably to their helpless end. Their rope did not hold.

Though there are no remains, it is not inconceivable that some of them once sat by the delicate little lake below Denison Crag at Stacks Bluff in Tasmania and waded in the soft grey/blue clay under the still waters. It would only have been a visit to sip the water, to bathe.

The boulders surrounding it are too big to enable the transit of game, and there is no grass for the wallaby to eat.

Now climbers occasionally clatter and boast there. Between visits, the dolerite-lit air is quiet and cool, the breezes soft, and in the winters' cold, climbers may clatter again in their selfish pursuits.

I last leapt from boulder to boulder there nearly 40 years ago. The last Aboriginal visitor maybe 180 years ago. Now you do the same in a different millennium, you self-absorbed little prick.

What are you in youthful abundance but another bit of skin that passes by and believes it is important? We are but impermanence. Stone is as close to eternity as we can imagine and yet the mountain we know as permanent dolerite was sandstone about 40 million years ago and then the dolerite rammed into the stone below the landscape in vast molten sills, then the sandstone above washed slowly away and then an ice age poured millennially slowly over the mountains and one small glacier dug a small depression into the sandstone below Denison Crag and then retreated and disappeared.

So the Plangermaireener tribe and their predecessors passed by for 20,000 years or more with not a thought for scaling the cliffs.

And so you find yourselves here, stunted items of hope and confidence, racking up, spitting, gunning for one small ascent after another.

...

Some people chatter and laugh, smoke drifts from their clay fire-carrier, they dip their fingers in the lake and renew smears of ochre on their skin, refresh clay and ochre packed in their hair. A small boy falls among the boulders and cries uncontrollably. He has torn flesh off his shin on the rough dolerite. The blood fades, the skin dries and floats away. In 40 years' time Anthony Cottrell will round him up for George Robinson whose claim to a place in history is that he worked earnestly and capably to eradicate a people and a culture. But the boy does not know this yet. Not in 1794.

...

Peter (Mungrl) Reynolds came with us when we climbed some early routes there. He viewed a can of Coke and a packet of fags as the sum total of sustenance required for a day on the road. He took a few photos and hung around as good mates will, looking forward to the evenings by the fire.

His name is on some climbs around the place. They won't be hard climbs. But he climbed them first with us and with others. Don't you dare deride them. He left some skin on the rock. It dried and floated away.

He sits beneath Druid and Blue Eyed Sun as we do the first ascents and takes black-and-white photos with my old camera. A day in the Tasmanian sun that passes and slowly disappears. He will one day fall and the rope will not hold him. But he does not know this yet. Not in 1972.

...

The plaque that hides his ashes in Cornelian Bay Cemetery in Hobart looks up at the Lost World cliffs on Mt

Wellington where we passed some good days. He left behind a few names attached to climbs, a few badly taken photographs and a buttress named Mungrl at Stacks Bluff. The Coke and cigarettes long gone. Now he shares just plaques and graves. Poor company for a good bloke. Pour some beer on the ground if you pass by. He'd like that.

...

Some music is playing but I can't quite hear it. I think it's Mussorgsky, maybe it's Cage. Walk by, reader, walk by...because that's your music playing. It's 40 years from now and someone is deriding what you achieved. They have taken your name out of the guidebook and replaced it with their own. They think the climbs you put up in 2008 are ridiculous. They have removed the bolts and view the attitudes of this decade as laughable. They think the end of their lives is an eternity away, that they have the length of time to make their mark on the world.

They know not what they do.

...

Bob McMahon at Stacks Bluff, Tasmania, 1971

The history of the world

The Trinity - No Blind

As I awoke one morning the history of the world passed through my mind.

Now who amongst that panoply of notables, I wondered, lives in memory among us even now, whether bloodied or gilded by their deeds?

It is the slaughterers and the claimants to godhead who are seared in memory. Genghis, Napoleon, Alexander, Jesus, Mohammed, Buddha. I guess that means no-one will mention my name in a thousand years' time.

…

When I was 14 my grandmother said to me that her life's achievement was her grandchildren. It seemed to me, false idolator of my life's potential greatness, that that was a paltry thing with which to mantle oneself.

My signature would be stamped across the face of the world and they would know me by my deeds.

Funny though. I don't remember the decades passing with quite that result.

…

Yesterday I received in the post Jerry Narkowicz's *Climb Tasmania,* an excellent guidebook to the best of Tasmanian routes. Like any fool, I went straight to the pages that referred to me, and cold blasts of yesterday soon shivered slow through my bones.

Again that blizzard of loss and bemoaning. Pastures of plenty spattered with passing time, unseen opportunities, missed trains, over-grey forests.

…

I am sitting on the rocks at the Lake Valhalla campsite below Stacks Bluff. Peter (Mungrl) Reynolds, is laughing, dick-deep in the water. His feet in that soft, light blue-cream sludge coating the base of the lake surrounded by dolerite boulders. Dug into the sandstone below by the little glacier that could.

Ian (Lew) Lewis, and I are lounging by the tents after our first little adventure among the rolling vertical prairies of unclimbed dolerite—Druid, 170 m, 17.

It is 1972. We are blissfully unaware of Tom Proctor at Stoney Middleton and just how far we are behind the climbing world's cranked-up future.

…

A trinity of soaring lines beckoned the days ahead. Each of the three lines, side by side, 200 m straight up and down.

Another day later and two were climbed. Long days. Clinging to small holds, deep cracks. A thin blade between the day and whatever else there was.

Bryan (Hooks) Kennedy, appeared and I had to race off to meet Maddison, Carrigan, Dunstan et al for a fruitless excursion to Frenchman's Cap. 'Joe's little boys'. That's a phrase very much of its time, and I use it advisedly, as a term that perhaps 20 people alive today will recollect and understand. It is part of a mystery that serves only to enhance one's sense of fragile individuality, of belonging to something unique and shared, and completely, stupidly forgettable.

Not quite the destruction of civilisations or the creation of global religions.

…

Permanence, impermanence. Now it is today, and yesterdays are turned to guidebooks. All those paltry climbs, those pissy importances. We are become as important as the ugly centurion at Vindolanda, the crippled miller at Avignon, the bloated Tyrean seller of purple. The unknown and unimportant people. Unrecorded bubbles on the sea's wide and plentiful surface. Remembered, if at all, only by DNA's uncaring persistence. Sparks that die soon after their moment appears.

...

We create in stone, yet are ephemeral—even Bob
McMahon in Tasmania, Chris Baxter in Victoria and Mikl
Law in Sydney, new routing with admiral consistency over
decades. When the next ice age comes and the guidebooks
are all returned to worm food, their souls will not fly on the
wind and remind the future of how they passed their long,
compulsive days.

...

How will time view us? Eroded aluminium found in cliffs.
Plastic boots and bones discovered in glacial debris. There
will be no names. No climber will be celebrated with
pyramids.
We are fodder for time. Feeding on climbs with fragments
of civilisation's muscular imagination.
The wind blows through the guidebook and shivers my
numbness. The bubble bursts and the sea remembers
nothing. The cast-off skin blows off the hold and I am not
remembered by the stone I dared to see as my new route,
my vast and crapulent pyramid of eternity and glory ...
become a zephyr of yesterdays, a puff of petulance, a
whisper of when, and why.

...

Dancing with shadows

The Trinity - Aqualung

Memories become shadows, indistinct, miscoloured. Lew belaying me in Druid. No, that is an old black and white picture. McMahon grunting up Ach! No, that's a picture too.

Racing Reg Williams across the Stacks Bluff boulder field, easy climbing in screaming winds with Bryan Kennedy on Typhoon Ridge...memories at last.

So I plough back through 36 years to 1972, put the pictures away and I find me, Mungrl and Lew still teenagers. My third trip to Stacks Bluff, their first. I had wittered on about these three lines I had called the Trinity—three pure straight lines one beside the other, 200 m high. That was why we were there, pure and simple.

It didn't rain. It wasn't cold or windy. We climbed. They were my best friends. Bob Dylan and Captain Beefheart tapes banging into the evening from my old mono tape player by the fire.

Lyle Closs leading the first pitch of Druid (16),
Mungrl Buttress, Stacks Bluff, Tasmania, 1972

We did an easier climb first—I have the pics but had to be reminded what we named it. 160 metres or so of delightful blocky dolerite, ambling upwards via the easiest route we could find. Druid, 16 on Mungrl Buttress.

Then it was onto the Trinity.

I can't remember anything about Blue Eyed Sun. We climbed it. We thought it was 17. It didn't pose many problems. We must have been more comfortable with long runouts then, because in my pics the gaps between runners seems inordinately long. Of course, we were probably still using mainly Ewbank crackers—solid aluminium hexagonal bars drilled through for tape or rope. But I put the pics away.

Next day it was No Blind, 18. I backed off the crux despite Lew's urging and was at least pleased when he got there and admitted it wasn't easy. But then, of course, he slammed it anyway. That memory at least clings on.

Then I had to leave to meet a group of NSW climbers who I had agreed to go to Frenchman's Cap with - Ben Maddison, Dick Hain, Matt Dunstan, Kim Carrigan, Bill Wilson.

Bryan Kennedy had meantime walked in to join Lew and the next day, while I messed around in Hobart, they climbed Aqualung to complete the Trinity. They graded it

19, while today consensus suggests 21. That makes it easily the hardest climb in Tasmania at the time, probably the hardest multi-pitch climb in Australia.

I should have stayed for the third line. I really should have stayed. In a life there are few such opportunities. It didn't seem as important then as it seems now, when I am 54 and dancing with shadows.

...

You sneak up behind someone and scream in their ear. They jump in the air and land awkwardly. They seem a little different. A little crumpled, a little blunted, interrupted.

Stacks Bluff slammed before my eyes like palsy—blind men laughing, assuming the world will always be blinded. I was that dumb and glass-eyed other person when Ian Lewis slammed the door on the Trinity. That palsied partner wanting to touch the stars but stymied by small towns and surrounding waters, always wondering what else there was and never quite defining it. Wanting to escape and not realising that the best escape was to let the limbs flow, let the dolerite sing. That weakness, sadness, dereliction could so easily have been segued into glory with just the dumb application of forearms and insipid inspiration, hold to hold, grunt to grunt, glory to beatitude to perfection within the space of a single route, a few dumb idiot strokes of flesh on Jurassic permanence.

So I walked away, left behind the illimitable resonances of climbs I could have climbed, days I could have passed in the pressing of the flesh upon the impermanence of the ticking watch.

Stop. A hand is jammed into a crack at Stacks Bluff. The body easily held. Nineteen and fluid, compressed, a clock spring desperate for another season. Fearful, watchful, wishing it flowed more easily. Trying not to be scared, but then the pitch, the lead, the flood of blood and heaven sluiced into veins, the genuflection before eternity before the cock crows and mere humanity collapses at your toes at the end of the climb. You are become man and man is weak and man is putrid and into the mind floods the knowledge of apples and sex and finality and you beg for life and more of the same that is the crux just past the adrenalin that masks itself as deity cuckolding your perfection with subtlety, with plastic divinity, with an ache that tattles itself as more than the small geography insists on. Then it is night and Hobart is a gorgon.

Stacks Bluff 34 and 36 years ago. Too easy. Just climbs. Just things done when the world seemed endless and there were summers ahead when everything would be done.

Angry, no, oh no. Regretful, well, a little. Delighted, yes, to have had those summer days when most of what we know was unknown. But a sense that one ought to be getting into a fight now, that one ought to have made a bigger stamp on the universe, however small that Tasmanian climbing universe might be. That was one's tribe. One's tribe. That one left the tribe and made no other mark, when marks are all that one can leave behind. That Bob McMahon and Stefan Karpiniec and possibly just a few others have decently maintained the early 1970s tribal markings we share, the flimsy scratches on the planet's stone. Where paper dissolves too quickly. Where time is a humour unsatisfied. Where permanence becomes shade and shade becomes seconds and we are but the sound of a falling stone in the universe's long, long decline into entropy.

...

We were just boys

We were just boys. What, for god's sake, were we doing attempting to climb a 300-metre vertical cliff straight out of the sea with no experience, paltry gear, and nothing by way of adult guidance. Such is spring,when saplings think the rainforest owes them greatness.

My mother drops Ian Lewis, Rob Craske, Jeff Burgess and me at the roadhead and says she'll pick us up in a week. What was she thinking? "Will I ever see my son again?", "I hope they have a nice time", or maybe "Have I got everything for tonight's dinner?"

The dry, dusty, eucalypt scent of Tasmanian country roads rises to greet us. Fat banksias prod into the dissembling air that promises great things. We hunker bulging packs onto already sore shoulders and grunt with dull resignation. Then we are figures strung out along a bush track, urgent, serious, wondering.

The Chasm is Tasmania's highest dolerite sea cliff. It plunges from 300 metres the top of Cape Pillar straight down into the sea, and there may be another 50 metres of cliff below sea level. Two high walls meet at a chasm which axes into the cape, pounded most days by big seas

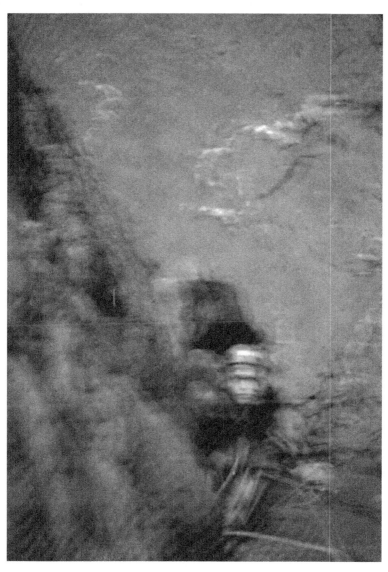

Ian Lewis following on the second pitch of the first attempted ascent of The Chasm, Tasman Peninsula, Tasmania, 1971

The picture quality is poor, but a reflection of how we felt.

and occasionally by monstrous storms hurtling in off the Tasman Sea. On rare days the sea is quiet and laps meekly on the dolerite columns, sentinels of Tasmania's geologically vibrant Jurassic past.

We sit that night by a small fire at Perdition Ponds, a campsite remarkably sheltered under wind-blasted casuarinas, just 50 metres from a cliff-edge as the long, narrow and steep cape pushes its way out from Tasman Peninsula. An hour or so's walk from the Chasm, Perdition Ponds is a place to relax, imagine glories unclaimed, swear unceasingly and fart whenever possible. My old tape player hammers out Son House and J.B.Lenoir and we sip a small supply of cheap port, unwilling to bring a hangover into the next few days.

The morning is warm and clear. Airs waft into the casuarina stand and shift the steam from our billy. We scrape the burnt bits off jaffles and blow on the steaming cheese and baked beans. Black tea and a two-day growth, with little stubble to show given our immaturity. I am 17, Ian 15. It is 1971. No-one has climbed The Chasm and we are damned sure we want to be first.

There is a line that goes from the sea to the summit in one narrow, unbroken crack. The rock looks smooth, and we assume it will require artificial climbing. We have read all we can about Warren Harding and Royal Robbins and think we know how to aid climb. We think we have geared up appropriately.

We gather what we have and saunter out to the top of the Chasm at the end of the cape. We lie at the summit and look down to the sea. It is a long, long way down. As the day rolls on, Rob and Jeff decide to head back to Perdition Ponds. Before they go I lay out our climbing gear on the ground and take a photo, just like photos I had seen from Yosemite before big aid climbs.

We shake hands solemnly and their shadows blend into the bush.

As the day fades, Ian and I scramble down the steep gully east of the Chasm to 30 metres above the sea. We scrape small platforms in the steep dirt, eat an uncooked meal, and lie down to sleep. We begin to feel the enormity of what we have taken on. The cliff spires into the dark. The sea rises and sighs, rises and sighs. Then the lighthouse on Tasman Island begins to rotate through the sky... whoomp... whoomp...whoomp...the long arm of light thunders under limp clouds, drenching the night with wave after wave, warning away the foolhardy, threatening disaster to all who approach. We hardly speak, and hardly sleep, anxiety amplified by the pulse of the unspeakable.

In grey early light we sip water, eat lightly, organise climbing gear on slings about our bodies, and stash extra clothes, food supplies, water and spare gear into my home-made haul-sack. Light green canvas with haul loops and rucksack straps, double sewn and riveted.

We hustle down to the lapping water, on ledges that step down and across to the edge of the deep waters and soaring columns. What else can we do but execute the plan, begin the climb? What other option could there possibly be? We are just boys. Bristling with expectations that life was like a fireworks display, you just had to light a fuse and great things would happen. We had lit the fuse. What option did we have?

The line we want to start on is five metres left of the last ledge, out where the rock spears into the sea. We'd rather not start with a swim, so Ian sets up a belay and stands by the pack with rope in hand while I prepare to climb.

For us, in 1971, belaying means the rope runs from the climber to one of the belayer's hands, around his back and to his other hand, both protected by leather gloves. If the climber falls, the belayer grips the rope tightly around his back and waist, the leather gloves taking the burn-inducing friction before the rope comes to a halt. We are using laid nylon ropes, less flexible and more friction-inducing than the soon-to-be-available kernmantel ropes that are now the norm.

I climb out and up to a narrow ledge, traverse the ledge, then lower myself down to footholds and climb across to the base of our long-dreamed line and set up a belay. It seems a fearful place, whelmed by vast grey walls, the wallowing sea under a dull, grey sky, and the regular bass thump of the low swell into the Chasm's wine-dark cave. Ian follows clumsily, carrying the heavy sack, and gratefully hands it to me to hang from the belay. The crack is shallow, welded up at the back from salt-erosion.

The corner is a little less than 90 degrees, awkward.

Ian gears up, adjusts his glasses, and begins the climb. It becomes apparent fairly soon that it could take a long time. We don't know about the use of a 'cow's tail' to enable the leader to stand higher in the home-made etriers and so place more widely spaced gear. We do not have sit-harnesses, just waistbands made of two-inch nylon tape and tied with a tape knot. For big wall aid climbing, we do not have a lot of gear, especially nuts to fit into wide, shallow cracks.

Ian starts to run out of gear after 10 metres so belays at a small ledge and I prussik up to join him. It is awkward getting past him, but eventually the pack is hauled up and tied to the belay and I begin the slow upward movement above. We are not very far above the sea. I am working at not being too freaked by the seriousness of what we are doing and where we are. We have no way of contacting the outside world – mobile phones have not yet been invented - and the world we are in is grim and intimidating, and we don't seem to know what we are doing. Or maybe we are all too aware of what we are doing.

I stop after another 12 metres as my gear begins to run out. It is a hanging belay because there are no holds. I sit in my home-made sit-sling and call 'On belay'. Ian dismantles his belay, ties the sack to the end of the main rope and prussiks up, cleaning the paltry line of gear as he comes.

As he reaches me, he looks up at the belay, winces, and says 'That's a bit light on isn't it?' It seems pretty solid to me. A good placement of a large nut. Just one nut, taking all my weight, our sack, and Ian's belaying weight. What was I thinking?

Eventually we get the sack up, and Ian climbs above me, one carefully placed piece of gear at a time. After another 12 metres he gets some gear in at a point where the corner is again less than 90 degrees. I prussik up to beneath Ian, and it's a crowded angle in the cliff. I will not be able to climb past without climbing over him. We agree I will bang a piton into a shallow crack in the wall to get past.

I hammer the peg and half its length goes into the crack before it bottoms out, but it seems solid. I tie it off with a short sling, clip into the sling and step out to hang on the wall. I do not clip myself to Ian's belay. We were just boys. It is easier now for us to haul up the sack. We haul and I take the weight on my peg. Haul, take the weight. Haul, take the weight. Haul, take the weight…

…then my piton spits out of the wall and I fall.

I grab a rope with my left hand and shred flesh down the rope at speed. The sack falls. Ian grabs every rope he can see. I stop falling with a bounce.

"Fuck!" is the best sentence I can assemble.

"Look…" Ian yells down at me, and I turn over and see the sack three metres below me, haul loops ripped off, peeled open like a sardine can, the contents exposed but saved by the plastic bag inside the sack. It has counterbalanced my fall but is likely to upend everything into the sea at any moment.

"Are you all right?"

"I've burnt my hand really badly," and the pain starts to overcome the adrenaline. Parts of my palm and fingers look like meat pulp.

"Can you tie on there?"

What happens next is a blur. Somehow I get some gear in and tie on, gingerly lift the sack up and tie it together with some tape. Ian sorts his belay and abseils to a ledge below us, just above the sea. I lower the sack and then myself to the ledge. Ian ties to a rope and swims to the ledge we had left a few hours before, then hauls the rope in as I swim across with the sack, trying the keep the contents dry as best I can.

The sea sighs and washes below us, and we later agree that what we feel is not frustration at ambitions denied, but a vast wash of relief. Fear's grey predators had been loosed by the night's warning beams and looped by grim grey walls and the slap, slap, slap of siren waves calling. But here we were drying in the sun, alive.

I found a triangular bandage in the first aid kit and wrapped my hand as the first aid course had showed me. We packed up and slowly hauled ourselves up the gully to the summit and the walking track, my wounds throbbing madly.

The next day, even in the sheltered campsite, we could tell that the wind had picked up. After a meal and a cuppa, we put on jackets and walked out of the casuarina shelter to find an extraordinary wind howling in from the sea. As we cautiously approached the cliff edge we could see the wind hurling debris from further down the cliff into the air. We threw a dead branch over the edge and it was whipped 50 metres into the air and way behind us by the force of the gale. Rob tossed a flat rock out over the edge and it hovered before us for a second before sinking slowly away. It would have been suicidal to walk to the cliff edge. We crawled and then wriggled the last feet before risking a look over the edge and beyond.

We could see the Chasm. Huge waves were crashing into the rock and the spray was reaching two thirds of the way up the 300-metre wall.

If we had continued climbing, we would have been inside the spray, if not inside the waves.

Sometimes things just work out OK.

...

Lyle Closs returning from the first ascent of The Wick on the Candlestick, Tasman Peninsula, Tasmania, 1971

47463892R00066